For Angela
with love and all be

animaculture

Hilary X 18-7-97

To Rowan and Biddy

animaculture
hilary llewellyn-williams

seren

seren is the book imprint of
Poetry Wales Press Ltd
2 Wyndham Street, Bridgend, Wales, CF31 1EF

© Hilary Llewellyn-Williams, 1997

A CIP record for this title is available
from the British Library

ISBN 1-85411-202-3

All rights reserved. No part of this publication may be reproduced,
stored in a retrieval system, or transmitted at any time or by any means,
electronic, mechanical, photocopying, recording or otherwise
without the prior permission of the author.

*The publisher works with the financial support of the
Arts Council of Wales*

Cover image: 'Messenger' by Anthony Goble
1997, watercolour and handmade paper, 43 x 33 cm

Printed in Palatino
by The Cromwell Press Ltd, Melksham

Contents

Animaculture

The gardening angels tuck their robes
into their belts, pull their boots on
cover their heads with haloes and set out

to cultivate the world. Each one
has hoe and sickle, spade and watering-can
and wings, and a small patch

to care for. They come in all colours:
dawn, rain or dusk, rose, marigold,
moss, midnight; gliding between

reflections, rarely seen. At three
years old, occasionally I'd catch
the flick of a wing, a glitter on the air

a tickle of warmth behind me, someone there
playing roll-in-the-grass with me
pushing my swing. And at night

my gardening angel laid her head
beside me, smelling of daisies,
and breathed with me. At my maiden flight

along our street, my feet grazing the privet,
past lamp-posts and garden gates, her voice
in my ear steered me and said —

This is the way to heaven, along here.
Since then, so many false choices:
knotted with weeds, I'm overgrown

and parched as dust. Who will open
the door to the garden, who will water
me now? Wise child, I trusted my own

right words, I knew the angel's name
and that death was part of the game.
I find it very hard to remember her.

The gardening angels prune and propagate
moving in secret through the soul's acres;
have I called on mine too late?

Whistling, she strolls in from long ago,
and she hands me the rake and hoe —
Your turn, she says; and I feel my wings stir.

Bagful

In your dream, you reach into my bag
to find it stuffed with hair.
Coils, hanks, skeins of black hair

nudge at your hand, a soft shock
like touching a furred animal in there —
but worse, this is loose, this is chaos

tangling your fingers, the damp filaments
that cling like algae. As you draw
your hand back, there is more, more:

nets, webs of hair, accumulation
of years, the brush-cloggings,
strands you find by the sink, the plug-pickings,

the hoover-spindle windings, the moult
on a towel, the broom-knots
twined into bristles, the pillow threads:

bunched-up, gathered, stored.
To think that so much has fallen from my head!
I could weave rugs from it, stuff mattresses,

mix it with clay and daub a whole house;
knit sweaters from it till my fingers bled,
hoard wigs of it against baldness.

You scoop some out, and shake it to the floor,
hoping someone will clear it up.
I will not; this is hardly my fault.

I have saved all my combings,
plucked them from the carpet, from the air.
If you must open my bag, that's your affair.

Making Babies

The child gives her mother a drawing of Heaven.
A blank place, empty of trees
and sun and houses; just that
lumpy cloud mattress underfoot and angels
shuffling through the cirrus
with wings askew, with haloes
balanced over their heads like upturned "O"s,
like jugglers' plates at the end of their spin.
One teeters nervously, struck rigid
on round feet studded with toes.

But this is God's show, and he upstages
all others. The child imagines him
darkbearded, genial, whistling while he works.
She explains this to her mother, who sews
cross-stitches in pink and blue silks
on a dollsized creamy smock, who threads
a smile all ready, her needle poised
before she's even looked. *There's God*
the child informs her, *making babies.*
In fact it seems he could be moving house:

surrounded by boxes labelled BLOOD, BONES,
HAIR, SKIN and so on. Here are his raw
materials: the Blood Box brims.
She's drawn him in the instant of his power,
a conjuror with something up
those bulky sleeves, to flourish
with a flash and pop! — then paeans of applause
from the stunned, golden hosts.
Her mother laughs. *You funny little girl!*
The child frowns, flushed. She knows

what's tucked beneath her mother's print
frock, what grows there; she understands
what blood is, and skin, and hair,
the speech of her heart on her pillow — but can't

translate it. How should she draw
the fat, packed world? — vivid as sleight-of-hand,
clumsy as that play about angels,
improbable as death or dinosaurs
or Heaven buzzing like a swarm of dreams
out there where anything goes.

Ursa

for J.L.C. and R.M. 1.5.95

Sleep makes you hungry. I could eat stones, leaves,
beetles, birch bark. These are my woods:
I recognise the tangle and muddy hollows, quick
rustle, the sun threading down like this.

I tread in warm slabs of sun. I flounder
to my knees in snow clumps, blue in the shade.
Winter shrinks back. My heart's dull step
has kicked into a run. My slack lungs swell,
unfurl like rubber wings. I'm awake now.

Look at me: I am bigger than before.
My body shakes with each stride. I lower
my head to the torrent, swallow green thaw,
let it cool my fire. I eat. Blood in my mouth,
sweet salmon flesh. Still I need more than this.

Through the dark time, I huddled in a hole
with my arms over my face, my blood slurred
thick in my veins, my tongue stuffed like a gag
in my throat. Sometimes my soul would claw
its way out and climb the great spruce
arm over arm toward the arclight

of the moon, and all the forest
hushed in frost. Or else on days of storm
it blundered from tree to tree, torn by the gale
into rags, flew about roaring. Blizzard. The din
of branches, like hunters closing in.

But I'm alive again. I am solid, wrapped round
in sleek black hide. My claws and teeth gleam.
You saw me shuffle up from the trout stream, turning
stones over, questioning the ground. I ignored you;
                                        my mind
is on something better, my mind is on treasure.

Something found only by digging, a glow in the dirt,
in the forest floor. Under rocks, under roots, what my heart
needs, what my soul feeds on. I will turn every stone
on earth, until I find what I'm looking for.

Drawing Down the Moon

First, clear a space for it.
The moon needs room to breathe,
to swell and shrink.
And don't just think of the white disc,
but the light around it.

Remove all rocks and stumps,
nettles and cabbages. Be
ruthless; this snare must be smooth
as a coin, and fine
as the skin of your eye.

Next, take a rope, and cast
your circle. May everything
in the ring attract moonshine.
Then hammer wooden pegs
around the shape, pulled hard

against the wind, which would carry
your garden, moon and all
away, if it could. Remove
your coat, and get digging.
Right down to the subsoil,

two foot deep in the middle,
shelving towards one end. Use
a level; if the ground tilts
your prize will spill. Heap the spoil
high to the south, for shelter.

Strew sand for a bed
and tread it firm. Ignore
your neighbours' sidelong glances
as you unroll stout polythene
to keep the precious rays

from running out.
Stretch it tight across the hole,
weigh it down with stones
and feed in liquid
to the brim. Stand back

in admiration. Wait
until nightfall. Say
the spell; and behold the moon
in your garden, swimming up
through nets of water.

Frost Pocket

The sky has been lifting and lifting
exposing new heights
of blue by day: and by night
the moon pushes through
swarms of invisible crystals
with its prow of light,
splinters of sky ice re-forming, splitting,

bright jagged mirrors. Cold
from beyond the stars, an invasion
entering earth, eating into the ground
glueing molecules, stiffening soil
to a new element, the fifth element: frost
that drives out all others.

The pond rings with a dull
note, its surface pleats
iced muslin; drowned weeds
in shreds of lace. Frost
creeps from the ground, through feet
to legs and bowels
trying for the heart. This is
how we became ourselves:

exiled in ice, keeping a spark
alive, a hot coal. We pressed
our palms to the rock to say
we have survived. We crawled
in the dark to blow embers,
making the painted creatures
dance. In flame their spirits
thawed and ran; till beyond
the snowline, the spring rains began.

A nuthatch raps and chatters.
Finches watch from the sticks;
the apple tree's streaked white
with lime. Filling the feeder,
scattering crumbs and water
I draw them here, make a warm thawed
centre, a hole in the ice
to breathe through; small garden
magic, repeated everywhere
enticing spring — succeeding, every time.

Behind the Waterfall

The waterfall is at its best today:
satisfyingly huge, it booms from its rock wall
in a curve of white sound —
an upturned river, fat with rain
dense with crushed water, a sideways pull
that draws the whole world.
Up close, you can feel a wet gale
sucking you in, tugging at the trees
whose branches dance away

and my children clamber and call.
I don't worry, they're big now, this is their
place, behind the waterfall
while motherly I stand here
on solid rock, to be someone to wave at
to witness their daring.
Their voices are lost in the clamour
of fractured water, of foam
fragments that change form slowly
as they fall, stretching like gum
in emptiness before smashing, reforming

running away. Through a mask of spray
I see them waving:
grey boy and lilac girl
fading and blurred, aslant
behind the torrent, unfocussed
billion tiny lenses dropping through time
and space, holding this moving shape
together, this strange attractor
through which we grin and gesture.

When my son suddenly hugged me yesterday
he had to stoop — a year ago
I stooped to hug him — and he felt light and cool
as rain on my cheek; then out

of my arms and up to his full height
still growing. And my daughter
though she runs like a child, under her lilac sweater
the shadow of breasts in this light.

The waterfall roars between them and me.
Fluid, unbreakable, a closed gate
of running glass through which
they waver and stand
beyond reach yet visible, mouthing
excitedly, deafened by the sound
of waterforms changing, exploding
escaping, unstoppable, sweeping us all
before it, downstream. And when, surprisingly
they return, shaking the thunder from their brains,
soaked through and laughing, it's like meeting
again, after a journey, after a dream.

Dandelions

My yard's unweeded, warm with dandelions
I will not cut away till they whiten,
honey-scented rays on worn stone
blazing bravely. Banished from the rich
green sterile fields, they crowd
the roadside like beggars, they loiter,
turning on passers-by their gold eyes.
Milk from their snapped stems stains dark
and bitter, they are no respecters of persons,
their leaves ragged and toothed, crude pissabeds,
long rooted, fecund, shameless. Yellow
gypsies, raggle-taggle, camped
at the margins, the city plots,
waste lots and motorway verges:
largely ignored. I've a kinship with them.

That's why I have sat with them
tearing yellow from green, yellow from green
for four hours, my fingers sore and brown,
for wine thin and sharp as a cat's stare
with a heart that burns small, gleaming
honeycomb heart. My daughter brings
a handful, bunched like suns
in her round fists. She squats hard
on her heels, black gypsy eyes
narrowing in the light. She grins,
and blows a seedhead, counting.

Star-gossamers float, touch
down invisibly on next-door's lawn,
needle between the blades, stitch themselves in.

In Her Own Voice

The sun is so exuberant. Even
in this cool room, it pushes its way through
the small deep window that holds out its wings
to receive it. Listening to you
here, in your living room, my eyes
are distracted by sunlight, and it seems
you're no longer in this house, but somehow
outside. We sit quietly:
the children eye each other, but make no sound.

Your voice advances, retreats. There's a fuzz
of static, a boom of wind
in the microphone. You speak alone,
but we all hear you. The air
crackles with attention; you've never talked
so freely to us before. I am watching
beech leaves uncurl, as you say
Almost nobody understands; and I want
to squeeze your hand, reassure you.

I am wearing your watch: I feel
its slow pulse work. The pin's at the last
hole, and still the strap shifts a bit —
my bones are narrower. Yours are chalky
grey dust in a dragon pot on the low table
under the sun. *Don't be afraid* you say,
*Everything will come right; but you must
believe it.* And at last you speak
of your husband, your love: he sits

bowed, his spine to the wall, eyes
shielded by his hands. The trees brim
with birdsong; your orchard blossom hums
and dazzles. In death, your arms flung out
in supplication or praise, he kissed you
once, on your forehead.

This tape has ended.
There's a shared exhalation: you're
elsewhere after all, calling us down

to the river, the outspoken sun, the world.

Mother Anthony's

Looking for the well in the wood
the named well in the named wood,
looking for a source, a spell
of water from rock, from soil
from the veins of trees —
and never quite finding it

we visited, we revisited
in all seasons, with the wood blown
and bare, or sappy and plush
full of voices, to discover
a stream without source, whose source
shifted from rock to swamp
to cornfield. What we found

wasn't the named well, but something
unnameable. A tingle beneath skin,
the way all paths led downwards
crouched under boughs. And the stream
stone cold, with a crushed taste.

Once there were hares racing
at dusk up and down the hill
as we approached, oblivious to us.
Once a thunderstorm
that pelted us from the trees
into the parched stubble of the fields.

We visited, we revisited.
We found a bottle buried in a pool,
old bubbled glass. Sometimes we drink
from it, toast Mother Anthony,
looking for what was lost.

Archaeology

That summer digging in the rubble
by the brick gasworks, spade by trowelful
in rectangles of string, sweat stinging
lids and with thin straps chafing
round brown shoulders as the sun blazed

and the taste of grit after a hard day
the smell of our bodies, still new, as we lay
together on a borrowed bed, too close
to sleep for great exertions;
a summer in history, the sweet hash smoke

at Naomi's, worn carpets, old silk shawls,
brown rice, bare blackened feet in the street,
freedom to sit on pavements and laugh
at the suits and high-heeled strutting —
that summer we uncovered the Saxon road

east of the town is long buried, long
ago died. And the girl with the strong
supple back and solemn gaze, exploring
the dirt in search of other lives
and nightly surprising herself in a strange place

is also dead. You may find her skeleton
curled in on itself, rubbed with ochre
waiting for rebirth, if you trowel deep.
For years I held her skull as a keepsake
behind my closed eyes. If you must,

dig carefully. Here are fragments:
the small bones, easily lost.
What I am now is only a storehouse
a museum of my selves, folded over
each other, strata on strata

and the hands that scraped Jutish
silt from her nails, and stroked
his dark skin are gone forever,
their cells sloughed off. Why should those years
be opened up, their layers reappear

except to teach us something? Was
there something I've forgotten, some vital
clue in the dust I failed to understand?
That site, covered up so fast. Is this
why you've turned up now, sieve in hand?

Changeling

for Peter Gruffydd

The marriage of wood and water
   spawned this creature:
wood chromosomes and water chromosomes
   juggled together

shaping a wizened femur
   as if old ivy-woman tossed her legbone
to the elements, and the waves took it

to scour the moss and the dirt away,
then rolled it back to the shore.

There are faces in it, gargoyles, girnings,
   the grin of a running dog:
an ivy-dog running from tree to tree,
   a sea-dog cocking its leg

at the suck-slick of the tide
   that whittled it
by the push and pull of the moon;

wood and water and the lunar carver
   conjuring a fake, a changeling
brat, a beglamoured stock
   outwardly whole

but inwardly skewed like this.
   I'd love to see the rest
of the skeleton: the ribcage opening
   its shrivelled petals, the pelvis writhing
in exuberant loops, the skull —

What would they make of the skull? The one
   true giveaway, that careful smoothing of flesh
cannot disguise. And of course it was
   by the eyes you knew them inhuman.

The goblin urge to recreate, to play
      with blocks of DNA, to make believe:
and we're part of the game

so an ivy stem can mimic a thigh bone
and our veins web out like a tree

with the sea moving in rhythm
      through us, casting us back
along with other flotsam, woodbones and shells
      in the tidal reaches

and who
      comes combing the beaches for what remains of us?

Above the Tide Line

Above the tide line
tucked into stalks of marram
stiff with salt, and old seaweed bundles
thrown at its feet, the gull lies back.
It is pillowed in sand.
Its wings are folded like hands
neatly and soberly:
grey sleeves drawn down
the cuffs crossed. Its head is turned
sideways, the shut bill yellow
as a flower, the breast still
gleaming, a curve of snow.

This morning sea and sky are one
film of grey light,
the air milk-warm.
A frill of surf folds itself under
as the sea steps slowly
away. The gull rests
knowing nothing of sea or sky
or movements in the slack pools,
or crimson foxglove towers, or this bee
that sails from ragwort to yarrow.
It offers one dark eye pit:
just a few flies exploring it.

The Undertakers

There's always the dead to dispose of.
They gather in drifts like leaves
they rustle in the dark with mice and spiders.

Allow them, and they'll accumulate
collecting dust, silting up the drains
scuttling over the ceiling with birdlike feet.

Someone has to hoover away the shadows
and clear the house. You can trust
us to facilitate everything:

we'll roll back the carpets, turn out
those musty cupboards, drive the moths
off into the night where they belong.

We'll respect your wishes. The remains
will look safely dead, not sleeping —
the eyes clamped shut, the limbs laid just

so, closed off, finished. Should you brush
the skin it will be cold as rain
and dry as feathers. You musn't grieve

too much. The dead are strong, stronger
than you'd expect. They'd like to linger
in doorways, or cluster like bees in your hair

footsteps following you everywhere. You'd meet
them round corners, feigning your reflection
in a shop window, hustling you on the street.

The living are so frail! You could be swept
aside like paper in a gale by those
who lust for life. It's our job to explain

that it's all over. Fold their hands together.
Bring in the flowers. Don't you mind the weather
these autumn gusts rattling the door:

there's nothing there. That's what we're here for.

Doing Her Roots

I

White pushing through black. A shining wedge
slid up from her skin, as if a live
tissue of silver grew under her scalp, a snowy

skullcap, putting out feelers, mycelium
climbing each strand. In the wind

the dark curls lifted: white slices caught
beneath them, slatternly, like the hem
of a slip that sagged askew.

However she brushed and rolled, it showed through.

II

Mother, always ahead, her heels chastising
the pavement, rap rap rap, her shoulders set
like knifeblades, the mothballed coat.

I dawdled and slouched, hauled after
on an invisible string. I trod on the cracks:
tried pretending I was not her daughter.

Following her, unwilling to take her hand,
watching the street breeze pick her locks apart

I saw her shrink and falter, suddenly old.

III

The bathroom ritual, with the door
shut. She on a low stool, her back
towards me, head below mine, bowed

in submission. Cold tiles: the china
bowl of black lotion, the rubber
gloves, the sponge. The ragged towel

of a penitent, a sinner. Her muscles clenched
against this, having to yield

her vanities to me, her imperfections
bared for my grace. I took the comb
and drew the hair into sections.

Dampened, it seemed thinner: the fleshy scalp
somehow unchaste. I performed absolution.

I was glad that I couldn't see her face.

What Brynach Saw

Carn Ingli, Pembrokeshire

Someone saw angels on this hill.
One of those early saints, the tough
weathered sort with big hands
and knotty calf muscles; the wild-eyed
sort gazing into a grey gale,
cloak bucking round him; rough
jowled, broken toothed from an old brawl
those nights before he fell in love
with the sky and became a saint.

A youth spent handling cattle,
hacking at stumps, cutting peat in the rain
to stack in low skewed rows
for the wind to dry. Planting beans, stooped
to earth; wrestling a boar down
for gelding in the swamp of the yard;
the screams, the stink, the swearing.
Brynach. A lad with a dusk thirst
no cask of ale could kill.

Parched, he longed to drink light
in bellyfuls, to feel clouds
surge through him. Watched swifts
dart and skim, watched the kite
hover. Fledged in the new religion,
discovered heaven as the mountaintops
sliced into his mind: dark blades
of ice, slipped scree. Here he stepped free
from flesh, from that long battle.

Alone with his love, arms out
to the sun like a heathen, he felt
the wind lift and hold him aloft
like the breath of God. From this height
the world is beautiful. You can carry it

all in your hands, the little stonewalled fields,
the sea leaping. You can see
what Brynach saw; how angels in the hill
raise their stone wings for flight.

Sculpture at Margam

for Deborah Jones, Miranda Whall and Olaf Probst,
Margam Park, Port Talbot: Oct-Dec, 1992

I. Maze Stone

Every corner you turn
brings changes: new views, or small
surprises. Back wall of a cottage
leaps up, displays
goddesses chastely framed
in elaborate archways —
always a shock
those beings in stone disguises,
the peasant's hut transformed to a palace of wonders.

In a dishevelled spot
past the glasshouses, October sun's
caught in a conifer garden
spicy-warm by the wall. Every step
leads somewhere unexpected
and here the path swerves

at a milestone on the road
to elsewhere. Humped and grey
with a hole right through it, and the loops
of a maze; a map
of your journey out of the mouth of the Green Man
who thrusts his leafy face
around the curve of the stone.
You can trace the way
with your finger, round
and back and round

to the centre space;
right through, and out
the far side. Like a lens
focussed on shrubs and ivy,
an eye made of air, a doorway:

not anywhere in particular
but here. Then return, dragging
your finger along the groove
that snakes and spirals
into the mouth of leaves.
This journey is endless.
In and out of the stone,
in and out of the trees —
the twisting roads of the stars
the maze in your brain.

Every turn, every path you take
brings you here again.

II. Stone Chrysalis

Something's going to rise
from the water. Semi-dormant
below the surface, something waits
locked in its stone
armour. Its crust is thinning
in the ripples, about to crack
open, split like a pod. I could run
my thumb along its spine and peel
it back to reveal
the image, fold upon fold
enormous, ready to stir.

But this is a work
of time, at its own pace.
Slowly the winged shape
creates itself from the inside
in secret, hiding its new
transfigured face. A breeze
chills the skin of the pond. Down there
under water, under stone, something
lives, and it's coming up
to meet us.

III. Capel Mair

Seen from the motorway:
skyline sentinel
roofless stones showing the woods through

facing the fumes, rattle and tackle
sprawled east to west
and the distant smudge of the sea.

Behind its back, the brown hills
rise and fall, moving
in to the heart of this land.

It's a gateway, urging us up
from the road's deadline
to the expanding circles of the world.

*

Why was the chapel built here
so high, such a weary climb
from the valley, such a trial
for old joints, for the mothers
of toddlers, such a trudge
through deepening snow into darkness?

Dusk comes early now, at the stub of the year.

Below, the abbey plumps out its skirts, queen
of its rolling acres. The grey brothers
held the green fields, the great church
in its echoing dusk; but the people
clambered through bracken and furze
for weddings, christenings, harvest —

the doorways of life. Here the seen and the unseen

meet. The park unfolds
like a map: the hills behind
are in the grasp of your hand.
Steelworks' smoke blows east; the roar
of the road rises, fades; and beyond
lies Devon, a shadow over the blade of the sea.

Heaven and Hell from here, and both cold.

So this is why the chapel stands alone
on the hill, to the Mother of sun
and snow whose place this is, whose rain
falls, wearing the walls away
letting in light and seasons. Old, old,
older than church or Celtic battlements

her shape in the land, river and tree and stone.

IV. Olaf's Stones

Giants brought them
   carried them like apples
in their aprons.

Six sinning sisters
   petrified
by the sun's rays.

Stone boat
   afloat on the hill
its nose to the sea.

A table, set
   with six places
for a feast of rain.

They walked here
   to look at the road
that was once a mountain.

Olaf chose them
   plucked them from the slaughter
the bone-crusher.

V. Miranda Brings the Sea to Margam

First of all, she cycled to the sea,
drawing a fine thread
from the copper trees;
under the motorway with a whisper
of spokes, a cobweb glitter

through the steelworks' grey
indifference, riding into
the molten sun, weaving a way
between hedgebanks to the shore.
Broad, empty sand; hammered water

curled towards her. She hooked
a scarf of surf and drew it up
tight; she spooled and locked
the sea-wind round her wrist
pulling it after, wound in her fist.

Back at the park, she propped
the bike, untangling
herself. Each holt and coppice
shone; but now, beneath the leaves
there's a tang of salt: the sea breathes.

*

Felt, the first fabric
from the age of ice.

Ice scoured these hills
lay like soap in the valleys

while women pounded wool
with grease and snow-melt

41

making hats and shoes
folding their babes in felt

the dead swaddled too,
under the ice, sleeping.

Miranda, surrounded by bundles
of combed wool, is making

felt to dip in the sea.
It smells of washday

as she scoops a soap solution
through an old net curtain

till the wool's sodden,
dissolves its oils, knits fast.

She wraps the sandwich round a wooden pole
cross-gartered with a stocking

squeezes, then unpeels the nets
and carries the sheets to the shore.

One by one, she spreads them to the tide:
dog-walkers, joggers pass all afternoon

as she hauls her salt catch in
and seasons it with copper, sea-green.

Now she has rolled the sea
like a carpet, and stacked it here

in small felt coils and cones
snug for the winter, as ice crinkles

the air, and the last leaves drop.

*

She says:
This is a work of time.

The Park is a clock
counting the hours

the tide-clock, the slow
pendulum of the sea.

The beeches have dropped their gold:
the flesh beneath blooms
with verdigris.

These new bright copper cones
will grow sea-green,
their pink cut wounds
healed over:

and the road-scar
and the city of oil and flame
will fade, and a skin of trees
will knit together

given time, and weather.

VI. Waterforms

December, and the park is made of water:
rustling, humming with water underground
and overground tumbling from the hills
caught in a ladle, tipped into the sea.

Trees made of water, in grey blurred rods;
the paths awash, the hillsides streaming
beasts stepping out of a lake, and soil
made of water under a film of grass
spilling over at each step. The pond
brims onto the walkways; the sluice
is deafening thunder. Even the air swells
and slides past, heavy with moisture.

Overhead, pale light swims round
briefly from dawn to dark. The pulse
of the earth is dull and sunken:
and yet this rain drives a new energy
into the park. So much speed and weather:
droplets racing together, the streams in spate
and rising; everything on the run

roaring, alive. To the south, the steel city
dissolves and softens in a fog of rain
and beyond that, lying in wait
for a small shift of the earth, another
spring: stones, trees, riverfuls of sun.

The Rose-Apple

They told us the double tree would be full of roses
come summer, the knotted apple
unpruned for twenty years in this dark garden
ruled by trees. We watched its early bloom:
starred creamy pinks, throwing crisp cotton prints

over the beds. Then browning, dissolved
to curls of soil, giving way to pursed buds
of roses. Nodding low in chains of briar
and curved thorns, laced with bindweed, ill-bred
nuisance got up in scarlet dots: nothing

to make the neighbours stare. But suddenly
one day was a scrap of red, caught high
in the tree, a fragment blown there
growing daily to a cluster, a crown, a rare
round dazzle of magenta, a cardinal's carmine

plump in the leaves, a rosebush dangling
thirty feet up. Through most of wet June
and through burning July it swung, fat
tree in the tree, a bees' bower, a proud
hat made entirely of flowers, a party balloon

that waved when the wind blew. And it grew apples
too: bunches of green pebbles that dropped
overnight like dewfall, the steep path underfoot
treacherous with their rolling; then turned them
yellow, streaked with rose crimson, waxed with sun.

On greenhouse afternoons we'd lie listening
to the rustle, thud and split of dropped fruit;
the banners of all branches strung with globes.
Beauty of Bath, an old variety, no more
in the catalogues. And no jungle-climbing roses

in the lists. The apples fall and spoil.
They need picking, but the tree's so tall, the stems
of the rose loop everywhere. Yet our neighbours recall
the old woman who lived here before, whose ghost
inhabits this place, who grew the shining rose

into the tree; how she'd take a ladder, and climb
and pull fruit, her husband standing square
on the ground with a bucket. And she'd crawl beyond
the ladder into the dipping boughs
scrambling in her skirt and plain apron —

a grey and greedy bird, her hands spread
to her fingers' tips. What faith or lust
held her steady in the air? Apple-lover, casting fruit
to her earthbound man, his face raised to climbing Eve
and the serpent-rose, wondering what to believe.

River Boulder

This is my resting place, the end
of my journeys. I am bedding in
more firmly with each season.

I've drawn back from the river
or has it drawn back from me? Its echoes

boom and rustle, magnified by crystal
but they don't assault me now.
That solid roaring speech that tumbled me
downhill, licked by its furious tongue,

that stunning weight of sound imprisoned me
in its flails and scoured me smooth
to its own shape, shape of perfected will

till I escaped the tyranny of water
for the rub of sun on my skin
the slick of rain
that gives me polish now.

I am a mountain waiting to become dust
— but there's no hurry. I've grown back
to a landmark, outwardly
immobile, all movement invisible.

And I've brought you up short, forced
you to stand, your unplanned goal —
warm fragment of the moving world —
your body against mine.
Hands brushing my lichens, pockholes of rain

as you lean, entranced by the river.
You'll walk no further
today, I've halted you

from the inside, freed you from time.

Green Gingham Wings

The girl, perched on the wall
like a sturdy bird
spreads her arms wide and sings.
She thinks she is unobserved

as she preens her wings
plume by plume in the breeze
that ruffles her skirt with the sound
of feathers. She stands inside

the bubble of herself:
the outer world wavers
bending the house, the trees
curved round a rainbow gulf

into which she leaps. She glides
a little way, then tumbles
and rolls. She's learning how to fall:
knees bent, taking the ground by stealth.

Is she the same child I saw
in a green check dress
flying over the heads of her friends
buoyed up by their cheerfulness

and the fabric wings she wore
strapped round her, a plump kite?
It was a short flight:
something snapped, the gingham tore

the strut broke over her heart
and she fell. They tried to mend
the dowel with sellotape, but the rest
just came apart. Now grown

bigger, she flies on her own
in all weathers. Dusk is best:
the blue air holds her further.
Soon, perhaps, she won't touch down at all.

Mr. Osborne

wore a black beret
snug to his small skull
(though berets were for girls). Wore
a greasy jacket, scuffed corduroys, a scowl
to set us running. A three-day
stubble, dark curls over the neck
of his summer shirt, a web
of wrinkles, a weasel grin.

Smelt of bonfires
after rain, and engine oil:
smelt of damp sheds, beery dregs
stacked in a crate, the insides
of gumboots, of just-dug soil.
Rolled cigarettes like dried
dough scraps with thumbs
as brown and nub as roots.

Drank cold fawn tea
from a lemonade bottle, spat
when he coughed, wiped his mouth
on his sleeve. Ate fat
white slabs of dripping-bread,
squat down in a square of sun
while we stared openly
half hungry, half afraid.

Chewed putty, so he said;
took the grey lump from between
his teeth, and showed us. Fixed
glass in the greenhouses
with stuff like plasticine
that smelt of the underneath
of tractors. Rolled it in lengths
like rubbery cigarettes, like pulled noses.

Spoke in a low rustle
that snagged in his throat
(we tried it out at home, limp
with laughter, swigging lemonade
like tea). Muttered to himself
round the backs of the brick sheds
shadowed by two children, who played
spitting, rolling baccy, chewing putty.

Under the Lake

Witley Park, near Thursley on the Surrey-Hampshire border,
was built by the notorious financier Whittacker Wright at the
turn of this century. The estate includes three artificial lakes, one
of which conceals an underwater ballroom, reached by a tunnel.

This was the lake you could walk under.
There was the dogwood lake, where a man drowned;
there was the fishing lake, where my father waited;
and there was the big lake, with its secret
swallowed in it. It had a mouth:
it had a stomach of glass, and a black gullet.

On summer afternoons it gathered light,
spread it between the trees. It lay
face to the sky, its skirts bobbing,
lily leaves and reeds in its finger margins,
snagged in its hem. Dragonflies stroked its skin.

I knew that smooth complexion was a mask,
the Queen who gazed in her mirror —
underneath, shadows rucked
and wrinkled into a frown.

The packed unbreathable dark went down
down, netted with weeds, with the bodies
of fish nudging blunt and cold.

I knew its sucking power. It dragged me
as I slept. The gulf of bad dreams widened

and I lost footing, and I toppled in.

Daylight, and I stood at the open door
to the tunnel under the lake

and the echoes hurried up
from the black pit, to greet me.
The lake's dark body odour: stone's

cold sweat, the outbreath from a tomb;
a fishy taint led to the sunken womb
the inner chamber. Cunt of the Lake Mother.
I wouldn't go down there. I listened

by the entrance as their feet boomed,
as their voices groaned and bellowed
from the bowels of the lake. I cried
for them until their heads appeared
across the water, mother, father, brother

on the viewing platform. They called
and waved to me, strangers, ghosts
from the other side, blurred and dim.
When they returned, they told me I'd been good —
but their smell was pondweed; their hands
brushed through the rising water, cold, like fins.

A Week Away

Falling asleep behind the folded door
I felt my grandmother lean into her chair:

I heard her needles flicker
through wool, the click of her cup

in its saucer, and I pictured
the blue veins purling her hands;

lulled by the warp and creak of the caravan,
the soft roar of the stove, the squeal

from her kettle, a whisper
of gaslight, the creamy sheet by my mouth.

But every night I dreamed of my own house
ablaze, burnt to a husk, crushed

by earthquake or explosion, cleft
with lightning like a tree

or filled with the thick green water
of the lake, and my parents drowned.

And once I found the rooms furnished with echoes —
they'd gone, and I was left.

Waking with snared breath and my face
wet, in a burrow of bedclothes

as my grandmother's footsteps moved
between supple walls, I'd lie

screened-off, a girl in a box, slotted
in place, and I'd listen to rain

drum on the tin roof, and hear
the slosh and clank of the enamel can

at the sink, and think of my family
shrunken by distance into blurred dots

that swam away from me. If I ever
saw them again, they'd be strange

and they'd smell of elsewhere: their eyes
would stare past me at another child

a little behind my shoulder.
And I'd find my clothes grown suddenly

tight, and myself much older.
Sometimes not even stone is strong enough:

when the people leave, the roof sags,
the windows crack, the house falls.

I used to feel I held the house aloft
somehow, by living in it.

This week, listening to the thin rain
breaking on someone else's tiles, I think

I've been away from home too long —
I shall return to find the house dwindled,

my hair brushing the ceiling, my elbows
jarring the walls, and everyone gone.

Deep Song

At school, we all sang soprano
sending our voices clear
through the tops of our heads,

our new-bloom women's bodies
ethereal beneath the stiff
pleated maroon

and as the notes flew up, we rose too,
hovering on plumes of pure sound,
the shriven vowels of nuns.

But between puppyfat and agelines
I lost that voice, I lost
all angelic strivings

visible now out of that uniform
of fluting descants, visible
and fleshly, having descended

to earth, my substance.
Now when I sing the sound rises
not from my throat, but lower,

from my centre, from the ground.
I've found my true voice in the register
of trees and stones and water:

so growing up means growing down
and deeper in. I've left heaven
to the birds with their child voices

while I rework the element of earth,
stir it with blood, with an old
unholy laughter. Listen:

the held note of the earth;
its pitched drone keys
all my music. This is my sphere,

its voice my voice.
I only visit the air
in rare dreams of a childhood spent there.

The Kindness of Women

for Anne Szumigalski

"Thou art the door of the chief of hospitality
Thou art the surpassing star of guidance...."
(from *Carmina Gaedelica*, trans. A. Carmichael)

An Englishwoman invites me
to her house along a street of trees
whose calm grey stems and darkdappled crowns
shade unEnglish whiteboard villas
dim verandas settling gracefully
to seed behind a mothwing flicker
of branches that almost brush their windows

in this far country

where I am a guest, escorted by this kind
ample woman with her softmannered voice
who goes before me up the many steps
to her porch, apologising to me
for the fading paint, the dusty unpruned shrubs

oh we have all seen better days

and in my dream we stand
in her diningroom before a vast table
of polished wood where an array of china
blossoms: small creamy cups, saucers
and teaplates sprinkled with scarlet flowers

an old service she says
left to me by my mother

displayed like treasure in this room
where warm light fills the open mouths
of the little cups, their daubed red blooms
so pert and cheerful, the clustered plates gleaming
across the broad oak and the woman smiling

welcome, you are so welcome

*

Will my mother leave me
her patterned china stacked
and graded like thin bones
in the mausoleum of her sideboard?

I always was so clumsy with her things
and stupid, not to be trusted:

it's only when I'm continents apart
I have the nimbleness to invent myself
as someone suitable to handle fine china
to enter an elegant oldfashioned house

discovering myself through strangers' eyes
discovering again the kindness of women.

*

A week after my dream I flew
to a country where spring was just
beginning its dance and the wind blew
from the rim of the world

and there I met my Englishwoman
pouring tea into china cups
in the open heart of the prairie —

and OK she was older than I am
my mother's age almost and her house was tiny
but solid wood brimful with plants and pictures
befitting a Queen of poets

her mind fierce but listening
her eyes magnifying earth and heaven —

I knew her of course by her mouth
luscious and full, the mouth of a young girl
whom life has not yet disappointed

and there was something stirring in the room
unfurling its fronds between us
the grace of whole souled loveliness
the grace of goodly speech....

How deftly she handled the teapot
being the chief of hospitality
and I the foreigner, a mystery

surrounded by emptiness and the sky rising.

Spring in Saskatchewan

for Jeanne Marie de Moissac, and many others

I. Water

Here they're called sloughs, pronounced slews:
springfed pools in the vast dry dome of the prairie.

Water that stands alone, watching the sky,
that makes a print of the sky; a film

moving over its lens, with clouds
blowing out and upwards, miles deep.

The earth opens, revealing the stratosphere,
the wind, the thinning air. Your face a shadow

featureless, as you lean against the light
to look in. We are blanked out by height

and depth and distance, silhouettes, little dancing sticks
on the broad flank of the world. The slough's

view: eyeless heads and peeled limbs,
a brief disturbance of vision. The white blur

of ice is gone, snow blindness. This is spring;
reed-tips prickle its skin. Its feathers ruffle.

Ducks settle over its heart. Its water-body
contains the whole sky. Out here at dusk

you can watch darkness seep along the land,
spread over the sky like paint; you can feel

the tilt of the earth, the roll away from the sun.
A great beast turning over. The sloughs its eyes.

This one, teeming with frogs, a cacophony
of sex and ecstasy, full moon frog rave.

The grit road a pale smear, rubbed out
by coming footsteps of night. Winter is over.

The land breathes, water sees, birds meet
and couple, frogs party, sky soars, the horizon uncurls.

Soon green will spike the dun stalks. Crocus glances blue
through sagebrush. Sweetgrass. This is the eye of the world.

II. Air

Six hours driving west from Saskatoon
over winterdun stubble a
dead straight road

do the dead travel like this?
with no thoughts of arrival, no sense
of direction, no curves
yet never bored, watching

that toppling pageant
cloud carnival inventing itself
continually, shaping, dissolving, remaking
always at the instant of creation

could be the otherworld, where everything
is suddenly clear

as I step out of the truck the wind lifts
and spins me like dust, snatches
my laughter like a scrap of paper

leaving me exposed to the white lens
of the sky, and there's nothing hidden
nowhere to hide, yet I can't stop
smiling and turning round

longing to fly, birdlike or even
cheating like Wisahkecahk who hitched
a ride with eagles and got terrified
and lost his grip: but what a view

he had as he fell
through stars, through clouds to ground!
the twirling blue

globe, the continents expanding, the ocean
rushing up in a dazzle, the prairie

bounding beneath him, reeds dancing like people
playing the first music, breathy and dry:

this whistling, this sound.

III. Earth

I brought two pebbles home from Wanuskewin.
One knucklesized, creamy quartz veined
in red, a rabbit's heart, a flesh nugget.
One to curl in your palm, dark flushed brown
sunset on stone, smoothskinned, firm, warm.
If you cut it, it will bleed. Thick ruby gouts
                    spreading over your arm.

Wanuskewin: *peace of mind.* Also, *to take a turn
in life.* The river turns in its valley.
I saw an eagle skim its broad curves
a few miles out of town, in the real world.
Omphalos of the flatlands, the swelling hills,
belly of earth. A birth was underway:
redstemmed willows quietly labouring
at their leaves, the tips just crowning.
Waters broken through the last membrane
of ice, folded their braided currents
over. By the creek Opimihaw
we watched a beaver in the brushwood steal
underwater, a russet glance and he was
gone. We took the path through the trees
and ferny hollows, past slow dancing reeds
up to the boulder land, across the downs
to visit a web of stones, the great Wheel
                    still invisibly turning.

But even in this place there must be blood
or the memory of blood; a bellow
held in the rocks. The buffalo
leap, outcrop of death, where the beasts flung themselves
as their running became unstoppable at the brink —
to lie brokenlegged, eyes rolling
waiting for arrows, or the stone knife.
Life to feed life. This, said the storyteller,

was what the people did. Sometimes they died
overwinter. Their bones fatten the land.
His eyes reflected shadow. His skin was smooth
                         as stone warmed in the hand.

IV. Fire

she walks out onto the deck
her washing basket heavily cradled
to meet the sun newly ablaze this morning
the sky flying a blue sheet over the prairie

we step down into her garden
what passes for a lawn is still hummocked with winter
the action of frost, but here are green blades
appearing like thoughts of summer

the day shivers with the promise of heat

she hauls her basket over to the line
today she will pin the clothes outside
show them to the sun

childrens' tights with woolly nubbles of wear
husband's denims dense and weighty as boards
cotton check shirts with frayed cuffs
underwear discoloured from months of washing
battalions of socks

side by side we peg them to the breeze
coldweather clothes, suddenly out of season

how intimately I am touching their lives!
her little boy's pyjamas, her daughter's slip
her husband's shorts, the small sewn towels she uses
faintly shadowed with blood

and now the telling of secrets, shaking them out
on the warm grass under the washline

afterwards she takes me to the pasture
we peel away our layers and lie down
the sun pours honey-balm
we are pale and cool, invisibly burning

the washing is dry by lunchtime

strange how you can burn without knowing
in the bare spring sun
so it's only when evening falls your skin flames

how summer comes in a day

V. Metal

Our last night, and the club is packed and dim
and very loud. A fine band: primed with sweat,
raucous with testosterone and whiskey.

I wonder at that bigcity sound in the prairie
this clapboard town — but of course the city
is everywhere now. It scoops us in

from suburb and stubble, from six thousand miles
across ocean and icefield — we share
its glitter and rhythms, leap in its net.

Twm and Iwan slip from boastful Welsh
to tipsy English, order more jugs of beer
whoop with delight at the sax solo

praise America. Monica, sheathed in gold
for poetry and parties, a Metis stunner
on a slow burn, remembers a lover

in the Aegean, the years when she was free.
Jeanne Marie, on leave from penning sheep
is here to dance; her laughing supple grace

summons us all. Tall Josef wipes his brow
and smiles, hot from the sweatlodge, stumbling
between two steps, electric blues and Cree

that simple, single beat. We're all in this
together, mouth to ear to hear each other
crushed in the din. Outside midnight cold

air clears the brain. A full moon.
Twm points, *lleuad*. Somewhere a ghostly train
rattles its bell, crosses an endless plain

into the dark. We are all far from home:
not only Twm and Iwan fumbling
sweet harmonies in *yr hen iaith*. Every one

of us on vision quest, unable to forget
the wilderness, yet laughing, dancing here
where spring and the city, midnight and music meet.

Notes:

Wisahkekahk: Cree Indian Trickster, who learned music
            and dance from the reeds
Wanuskewin: Native Heritage Park near Saskatoon
Metis: Mixed Native/French ancestry
lleuad: (Welsh) — "moon"
yr hen iaith: (Welsh) — "the old language"

A Nun in the Dunes

for Samantha Rhydderch

This woman has chosen coolness.
It fills her from toes to skull
an inner pool. It's behind her eyes
her pale coiled hair. The touch
of her hand is cold water.

A calm wind blows through her,
curls from her pores. She pulls on
flawless red boots. Fresh as rain
falling through leaves in a walled
garden, she's clean as dew

that appears all at once, a miracle
on the grasses. What she takes
in, she cools and stills:
the warm world, pressed in its frost
of linen, its iced silks.

She walked with us in the dunes
in the narrow sun of a winter
afternoon — a grace
without heat, being light only.
And being new to this place

she glanced round, birdlike,
at the hills of crushed shell,
spiked sloe and buckthorn, rags
of heather, and caught them all
to be smoothed, and folded.

I think she loves this weather,
the brief bright days. She could stand
on a mountain over the world
and wave a sword. The land
would fall in dunes like this.

We climbed a hill, stared out
over rainfilled slacks and gullies
to the sea. And God shone
in a cloud, descending to the bay
in rays of pale gold.

She took a picture, froze
the vision. Later she'll look
at it, framed in grey
on a white wall. She won't mind
leaving the dunes behind;

it's what she's chosen.
Cool air stirs round her
like a veil. I burn beside her
in my usual fashion:
my choice, my blazing grail.

Acknowledgements

Some of these poems have appeared in the following publications:

The New Welsh Review, Poetry Wales, The New Orleans Journal, Lyric (Shillong), *The Observer/Arvon Poetry Collection 1993, SW Poetry Competition Anthology 1991, The Urgency of Identity* (Triquarterly Books, ed. David Lloyd), *Drawing Down the Moon* (Seren, ed. Robert Minhinnick), *Intimate Portraits* (Seren, ed. Alison Lloyd)

and in the following HTV Wales programmes:

Grassroots (1996) and *A Word In Your Eye* (1997)

"Sculpture at Margam" was written on a residency supported by the Arts Council of Wales and Sculpture at Margam, Ltd.